The Best Way to See a Shark

By Allan Fowler

Consultants

Robert L. Hillerich, Professor Emeritus,
Bowling Green State University, Bowling Green, Ohio;
Consultant, Pinellas County Schools, Florida

Lynne Kepler, Educational Consultant

Fay Robinson, Child Development Specialist

℗ CHILDRENS PRESS®
CHICAGO

Design by Herman Adler Design Group
Photo Research by Feldman & Associates, Inc.

Library of Congress Cataloging-in-Publication Data

Fowler, Allan.
     The best way to see a shark / by Allan Fowler.
        p. cm. – (Rookie read-about science)
     ISBN 0-516-06032-5
     1. Sharks—Juvenile literature. [1. Sharks.] I. Title
   II. Series.
QL638.9.F69   1995
596'.31–dc20
                                                                94-36347
                                                                  CIP
                                                                  AC

They may look scary — but
not all sharks are dangerous.

Several hundred different kinds of sharks swim in the sea. But only about a dozen kinds ever attack people.

Some sharks are as small
as 2 feet long.

Whale sharks grow up to
50 feet long — longer than
a school bus.

Whale sharks are the biggest
of all fish. Yet whale sharks
are not dangerous at all.

Their food is plankton,
a mass of very tiny plants
and animals that floats near
the surface of the oceans.

Whale sharks never attack human beings. Divers can safely ride on their backs.

When people think of
sharks as being killers,
they probably have this
kind in mind — the great
white shark.

Great whites have even
been known to attack boats.

Look at those powerful
jaws and sharp teeth!

Tiger sharks, mako sharks,
and hammerhead sharks
are also very dangerous.

When you look at a
hammerhead from above
or below, you can see
how it got its name.

13

Most sharks are meat-eaters.

The bigger ones eat marine mammals — whales, seals, and dolphins — as well as fish.

And they will eat smaller sharks, or sharks of their own kind that have been wounded.

Does that make sharks bad or evil?

No, it doesn't. They are simply acting in the way that is natural for sharks.

Sharks eat to survive — and they certainly have survived. In fact, sharks have been around for many millions of years — since before the dinosaurs.

Most fish have bony skeletons.
But sharks, along with rays

and skates, have no bones in their bodies — just cartilage, which is what gives your nose its shape.

Most fish have scales.
So do sharks. But their
scales are like very tiny
teeth, so a shark's skin
feels rough and pebbly.

A shark has from 2 to about 20 rows of sharp, pointed teeth. Some of its teeth may break off, but the shark keeps growing new ones to replace them.

Sharks sometimes have "passengers."

A fish called a remora attaches itself to a shark's body. Remoras are 2 or 3 feet long.

24

They feed on what's left
over from a shark's meal.
They also eat pests that
live on the shark's skin.

Remoras that live on
sharks are called
sharksuckers.

Scientists can study some sharks up close.

But when they study the fiercer kinds, scientists must stay inside steel cages.

You may look at sharks up close, too, if you visit an aquarium or marine park.

That's certainly the best way to see a shark!

Words You Know

remora

plankton

ray

skate

great white shark

hammerhead shark

tiger shark

mako shark

whale shark

Index

About the Author

Allan Fowler is a free-lance writer with a background in advertising. Born in New York, he lives in Chicago now and enjoys traveling.

Photo Credits

Animals Animals – ©James D. Watt, 4; ©Ingo Riepl, 14
H. Armstrong Roberts – 21; ©Frink/Waterhouse, 24, 30 (top left)
Reuters/Bettmann – 28
Jeff Rotman Photography – ©Jeffrey L. Rotman, 6-7, 11, 18, 19, 27, 30 (bottom left and bottom right), 31 (top left and bottom); ©Itamar Grinberg, 9; ©Doug Perrine, 12, 31 (center left); ©Paul Humann, 13, 31 (top right)
Tom Stack & Associates – ©Dave Fleetham, Cover, 5
SuperStock International, Inc. – 3; ©G. Corbett, 31 (center right)
Tony Stone Images – ©Norbert Wu, 8
Valan – ©Fred Bavendam, 17 (bottom)
Visuals Unlimited – ©David M. Phillips, 8 (inset), 30 (top right); ©John Forsythe, 17 (top); ©Science VU-NOAA, 20; © John D. Cunningham, 23
COVER: Whitetip Reef Shark